The Story of a Special Day
Volume 44

February 13

The 44th day of the year. There are 321 days (322 in leap years) remaining until the end of the year.

by Michael Dobson

Timespinner
Press

This book is also available in e-book form for Kindle, e-pub devices, and other formats from your favorite online booksellers.

For more information about the series, about us, or about your special day, please email us at editor@timespinnerpress.com.

Look for other volumes in *The Story of a Special Day*, coming often. See www.timespinnerpress.com for details and for the most recent information.

Table of Contents

Cover: The 1916 St. Louis Giants National Negro League team (courtesy Missouri History Museum). The National Negro League was established February 13, 1920 — the COVER STORY.

Quote of the Day

"Men are more often bribed by their loyalties and ambitions than by money."

US Supreme Court JusticeRobert H. Jackson,
Chief US prosecutor at the Nuremberg Trials
born February 13, 1892

Today
in
History
February 13

Catherine Howard, by Wenceslaus Hollar

What Happened on February 13?

From the creation of great works of engineering and art, to devastating wars and natural disasters, thousands of years of history have left their mark on each and every day of the year. Here are some important events that occurred on February 13. (Illustrated items are shaded.)

1542 — Catherine Howard, **fifth wife of Henry VIII is beheaded** on charges of treason and adultery.

1689 — **William and Mary** become co-monarchs of England, Scotland, and Ireland during the Glorious Revolution.

1913 — The 13th **Dalai Lama proclaims Tibetan independence**, which lasts until 1951, when it is incorporated into the People's Republic of China.

1935 — Bruno Hauptmann is convicted of the 1932 **kidnapping and murder of the Lindbergh baby.**

1945 — The **Allied bombing of the German city of Dresden begins**. It becomes a subject of controversy as to its military necessity. Kurt Vonnegut, a prisoner of war in Dresden, chronicled his experiences in the book *Slaughterhouse-Five*.

1960 — **France detonates a nuclear weapon,** becoming the fourth nation to acquire nuclear weapons.

The Cuban Giants (1890), Cleveland *Gazette*

Cover Story
National Negro League Founded (1920)

On February 13, 1920, the first of the American-American baseball conferences to last more than a single season, the National Negro League, was formed in Kansas City, Missouri. It operated until 1931, when it perished under the economic pressure of the Great Depresssion.

Baseball, like virtually every other aspect of American life, was segregated by race. Nonwhites were excluded from Major League Baseball altogether, although a few African-Americans played on minor league teams until 1887.

In response, the first black professional baseball team, the Cuban Giants, began in 1885. They didn't actually have any Cuban members, but pretended to be in hopes of a wider audience. They were one of the most successful Negro league teams for nearly two decades. Other independent teams followed, the varying success.

The first attempt to create a professional African-American league, the National Colored Base Ball League started up in 1887, but only lasted two weeks. It was after World War I that the idea was revived, leading to the establishment of the National Negro League.

Other leagues followed, including the Negro Southern League and the Eastern Colored League. The Negro League World Series began in 1924.

Because Negro League baseball didn't have the same audience base as white baseball, the teams and leagues struggled. The Eastern Colored League gave way to the East-West League, and in 1933 a new National Negro League was formed, replacing the original, which had disbanded the prevous year.

Segregation in major league baseball continued, with first baseball commissioner Kenesaw Mountain Landis firmly opposed to integration. His successor Happy Chandler thought differently, and in 1945, the "color line" was broken when Jackie Robinson was signed by the Brooklyn Dodgers.

While the Negro Leagues continued, their day had passed. The last Negro League All-Star game was held in 1962. A single Negro league team, the Indianapolis Clowns, continued to play exhibition games as a sideshow until the 1980s.

A number of all-time baseball greats began in the Negro leagues. In addition to Jackie Robinson, such towering talents as Satchel Paige, Cool Papa Bell, and Willie Mays all were named to the Baseball Hall of Fame. The last of the Negro league players to have a regular role in Major League Baseball was home-run king Hank Aaron.

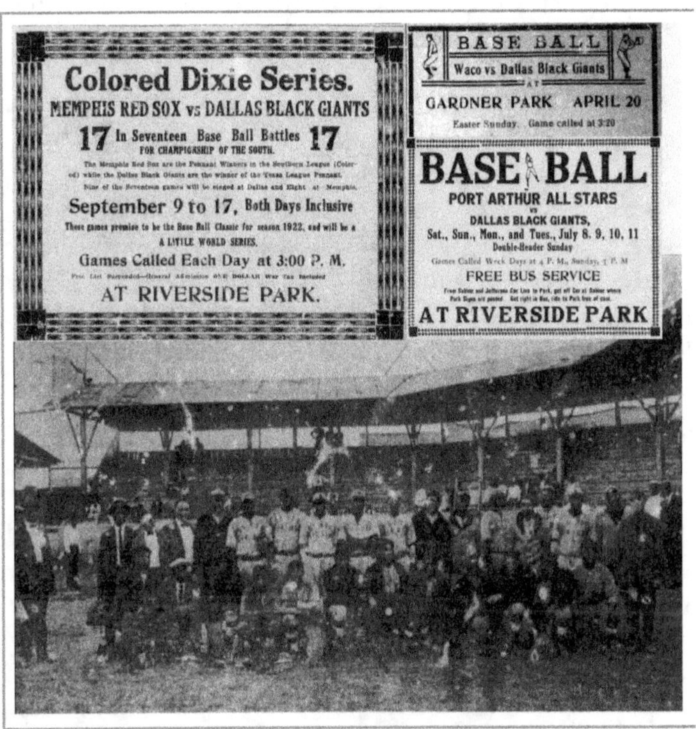

Dixie World Series of 1922

1960 — The **Nashville sit-ins**, a nonviolent campaign to end segregation at lunch counters in that city, began. Participants were verbally and physically attacked by white onlookers, and over 150 were arrested. Ultimately, the action was successful, and on May 10, 1960, six downtown Nashville stores began serving black customers.

1967 — Two **handwritten manuscripts by Leonardo da Vinci**, the *Madrid Codices,* are discovered in the National Library of Spain.

2004 — The **universe's largest known diamond**, a white dwarf star named BPM 37093 (later "Lucy," from the Beatles song "Lucy in the Sky with Diamonds.") is discovered. Its weight is 5×10^{29} kilograms (5 followed by 29 zeroes).

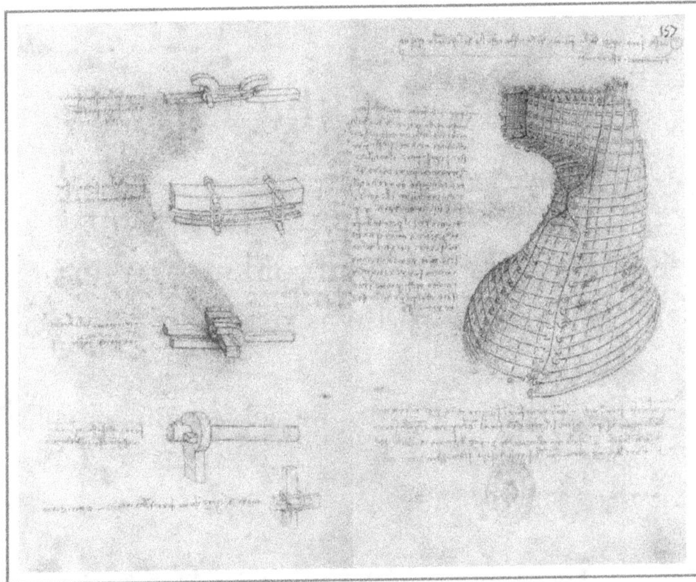

Pages from the Madrid Codices by Leonardo da Vinci

Quote of the Day

"He was born with a gift of laughter and a sense that the world was mad."

Rafael Sabatini, novelist
died February 13, 1950

Births
and
Deaths
CHEM
ACU
MAGNA
February 13

Robert H. Jackson (Photo: Harris & Ewing)

Notable February 13 People

With the current world population at about seven billion people, on average about 19 million people also celebrate their birthdays on February 13 — and that isn't counting the millions and millions who came before! No matter when you were born, you share your birthday with many special people whose accomplishments (and occasionally embarrassments) have been noted as part of history.

In this section, you'll meet fascinating people who share your birthday. They're organized by what they're famous for, and then in reverse chronological order from most recent to earliest. Those who are shown in photographs or artwork have a box around them. We don't have photos of everyone, so please forgive us if your favorite person is missing.

Some of these people you've heard of, others may be new to you, but they all make up an important part of the reason that February 13 is a truly special day!

                    Michael Dobson

American Gothic, by Grant Wood

Who Was Born on February 13?

Art and Illustration

Grant Wood, painter of scenes in the rural American Midwest, most famously the iconic work *American Gothic. (1891)*

Business and Technology

A.C. Gilbert, inventor and toy-maker best known for inventing the Erector Set. *(1884)*

An Erector Set motorcycle (Photo: Essig)

Government, Politics, and Law

Omar Torrijos, *de facto* dictator of Panama from 1968 to 1981. *(1929)*

Khalid bin Abdulaziz Al Saud (خالد بن عبد العزيز آل سعود), king of Saudi Arabia from 1975 to 1982. *(1913)*

Robert H. Jackson, American attorney and jurist who served as a Supreme Court associate justice, Solicitor General, and Attorney General, the only person to have ever held all three offices. Served as chief US prosecutor during the Nuremberg trials of Nazi war criminals after World War II. *(1892) (Photo page 12.)*

Bess Truman (right) with Harry S. Truman (Photo: Abbie Rowe)

Bess Truman, first lady and wife of 33rd US President Harry S. Truman. *(1885)*

Robert Malthus, political economist who argued that population multiplied geometrically, but food did so arithmetically, resulting in a Malthusian catastrophe. An influential and controversial thinker, his opinions had a major effect on economics and evolutionary biology. *(1766)*

Thomas Robert Malthus, by John Linnell (1833)

 Michael Dobson

Chuck Yeager standing next to the Bell X-1 in which he first broke the sound barrier. (Photo: USAF)

Person of the Day
Chuck Yeager (1923)

Chuck Yeager is best remembered as the first human being to officially break the sound barrier, when he flew the Bell X-1 "Glamorous Glennis" (named for his wife) at Mach 1 on October 14, 1947. He is widely regarded as one of the greatest pilots of all time.

Born in West Virginia, Yeager joined the US Army Air Force as a private during World War II. Initially an aircraft mechanic, he entered flight school and became a P-51 fighter pilot. He became a fighter ace, shooting down five enemy aircraft in a single mission.

Following the war, he became a test pilot at what is now Edwards Air Force Base. Following his achievement in breaking the sound barrier, he went on to set numerous other speed and altitude records. Later in his career, he commanded several squadrons and wings before becoming first commandant of the USAF Aerospace Research Pilot School, training future astronauts. (Because Yeager only held a high school diploma, he was not eligible to become an astronaut).

He was promoted to brigadier general in 1969, becoming vice-commander of the Seventeenth Air Force, and retired in 1975 after 33 years of active duty. He was portrayed by actor Sam Shepard in the 1983 film *The Right Stuff,* in which he made a cameo appearance as "Fred," a bartender at Pancho's Place.

Journalism and Literature

Georges Simenon, mystery writer best known for his fictional detective Jules Maigret. *(1903)*

Eleanor Farjeon, writer of children's stories and plays who won many literary awards in her lifetime. She is best known today for the children's hymn "Morning has Broken," famously covered in a hit 1971 version by singer Cat Stevens. *(1881)*

Music

Peter Gabriel, singer-songwriter initially known as the lead singer of the progressive rock band Genesis, and for his later successful solo career. His best-known hit is the 1986 single "Sledgehammer," the most played music video in the history of MTV. Also known for his humanitarian efforts. *(1950)*

Peter Tork, musician and actor best known as a member of the Monkees. *(1942)*

Eileen Farrell, American operatic soprano known for both classical and popular music; hosted her own radio show in the 1940s and released the first successful crossover album, 1960's "I've Got a Right to Sing the Blues." *(1918)*

Boudleaux Bryant, songwriter who along with his wife Felice wrote such hits as "Rocky Top," "All I Have to Do is Dream," and "Bye Bye Love." *(1920)*

The Monkees (clockwise from top left): **Peter Tork,** Micky Dolenz, Michael Nesmith, Davy Jones

Tennessee Ernie Ford, American singer and television performer best known for his 1955 number one hit, "Sixteen Tons." *(1919)*

Tennessee Ernie Ford

Performing Arts

Mena Suvari, actress and model known for her roles in *American Beauty, American Pie,* and other films. *(1979)*

Neal McDonough, actor known as Buck Compton in the miniseries *Band of Brothers,* as well as roles in films such as *Minority Report, Red 2,* and various Marvel films as "Dum Dum Dugan." *(1966)*

Pernilla August, leading Swedish actress best known for her collaborations with Ingmar Bergman; known to American audiences for playing the mother of Anakin Skywalker in two *Star Wars* films. *(1958)*

Jerry Springer, former Cincinnati mayor and attorney best known as host of the tabloid talk show *Jerry Springer.* *(1944)*

Stockard Channing, actress best known for playing Rizzo in the 1978 film *Grease,* and the first lady in the television series *The West Wing.* *(1944)*

Carol Lynley, former child model nominated for a Golden Globe for her role in the 1959 film *Blue Denim;* appeared in such films as *Under the Yum Yum Tree* and *The Poseidon Adventure,* as well as in guest roles on numerous television series. *(1942) (Photo next page.)*

Bo Svenson, appeared in several films in the *Walking Tall* franchise; also known as murder victim/ vigilante in the cult classic *Breaking Point.* *(1941)*

Carol Lynley

Kim Novak (Photo: Frank Bez)

Oliver Reed, English actor known for roles in *Oliver!, Women in Love, The Three Musketeers, Castaway,* and *Gladiator. (1938)*

George Segal, actor known for such films as *Who's Afraid of Virginia Woolf?* and *A Touch of Class,* and for the sitcom *Just Shoot Me! (1934)*

Kim Novak, actress best known for performances in such films as *Vertigo, The Man with the Golden Arm,* and *Pal Joey. (1911)*

Jean Muir, American stage and screen actress known as the first performer to be blacklisted during the 1950s "Red Scare." *(1911)*

From *A Midsummer Night's Dream* (1935): from left to right: Ross Alexander, Dick Powell, **Jean Muir,** Olivia de Havilland

Philosophy and Religion

Mirzā Ghulām Ahmad (مرزا غلام احمد), Indian religious leader who founded the Ahmadiyya movement in Islam. Often considered a heretic because he claimed to be the divinely appointed Messiah and Mahdi, in the likeness of Jesus. His movement today has between 10 and 20 million followers in 209 countries. *(1835)*

Science

William Shockley, shared the 1956 Nobel Prize in Physics for the discovery of the transistor effect; helped created Silicon Valley; later widely criticized for his views on eugenics and race. *(1910)*

Sports

Randy Moss, wide receiver who played 14 seasons in the NFL; holds the single-season touchdown reception record of 23 in 2007. *(1977) (Photo next page.)*

Denise Austin, fitness instructor and personal trainer known for her exercise videos and the television series *Getting Fit with Denise Austin.* *(1957)*

Mike Krzyzewski, college basketball coach at Duke University and coach of the US men's national basketball team that won gold medals in three Olympic games. Two-time inductee into the Naismith Memorial Basketball Hall of Fame, as well as the College Basketball Hall of Fame and the United States Olympic Hall of Fame. *(1947)*

Randy Moss (CC BY-SA 2.0)

Eddie Robinson, coached the second-most victories in NCAA Division I history as head coach of the historically black Grambling State University; member of the College Football Hall of Fame. *(1919)*

Patty Berg, all-time record holder for most major wins by a female golfer, helped found the LPGA, member of the World Golf Hall of Fame. *(1918)*

Hal Chase, first baseman and manager for several MLB teams, called by Babe Ruth "the best first baseman ever." Alleged to have gambled on baseball games and thrown games in which he played, and was eventually banned from the game. *(1883)*

David Janssen in *The Fugitive.* Janssen died February 13, 1980

Who Died on February 13?

Art and Letters

Josephine Tey, Scottish author best known for her mystery novels featuring Inspector Alan Grant. Her real name as Elizabeth MacKintosh; she also wrote as Gordon Daviot. *(1952)*

Rafael Sabatini, Italian-English author remembered for adventure and romance novels including *Scaramouche, The Sea Hawk,* and *Captain Blood*. *(1950)*

Albert Gottschalk, noted Danish painter. *(1906)*

"Early Spring in Glostrup," by Albert Gottschalk, 1887
(Courtesy National Gallery of Denmark)

Benvenuto Cellini, Italian sculptor and goldsmith best known for his famous autobiography. *(1571)*

Benvenuto Cellini

Business and Technology

Yoshisuke Aikawa (鮎川 義介), Japanese businessman who founded Nissan. *(1967)*

Government and Law

Antonin Scalia, associate justice of the US Supreme Court, noted for his conservative views. *(2016)*

Catherine Howard, fifth wife of English monarch Henry VIII; queen of England for 16 months before being convicted of treason and adultery. Beheaded at the Tower of London. *(1542) (Photo page 2.)*

Music

Dale Hawkins, singer-songwriter and guitarist known as a founder of swamp rock boogie; remembered for his 1957 hit "Suzy Q," which has been covered by many musicians. *(2010)*

Waylon Jennings, singer-songwriter who played bass for Buddy Holly before becoming a highly successful solo country artist. Memberof the Country Music Hall of Fame. *(2002)*

Lily Pons, operatic soprano and actress whose self-promotion made her a cultural icon. *(1976)*

Lily Pons (Photo: Ernest Bacharach)

Richard Wagner, opera composer best known for his four-opera Ring cycle (*Der Ring des Nibelungen*). Controversial for anti-Semetic views and for the Nazi appropriation of his works in support of their cause. *(1883)*

Performing Arts

Ralph Waite, actor best known as the father on the 1970s television series *The Waltons. (2014)*

Martin Balsam, won an Academy Award for his role in the 1965 film *A Thousand Clowns*, also appeared in *Psycho, 12 Angry Men*, and as Murray on the TV series *Archie Bunker's Place. (1996)*

David Janssen, actor best known for playing Dr. Richard Kimble in the 1960s television series *The Fugitive. (1980) (Photo page 28.)*

Mae Marsh, actress who began in the silent film era and continued into the talkie era; notable films include *The Birth of a Nation, Intolerance, Rebecca of Sunnybrook Farm*, and *The Robe. (1968)*

Religion

Lloyd C. Douglas, Lutheran pastor best known for his religion-themed novels inclding *Magnificent Obsession* and *The Robe. (1951)*

Mae Marsh, in *The Birth of a Nation* (1915)

Cotton Mather, influential New England Puritan minister best known for his support for the Salem Witch Trials, also made contributions to science and medicine. *(1728)*

Cotton Mather, by Peter Pelham

"February in the Isle of Wight," John Brett (1866)

Quote of the Day

"Life is what it is, and you take what's handed, and you work as hard as you can, and hopefully you'll be successful, but I just don't spend too much time worrying about that."

Jerry Springer, politician and talk show host
born February 13, 1944

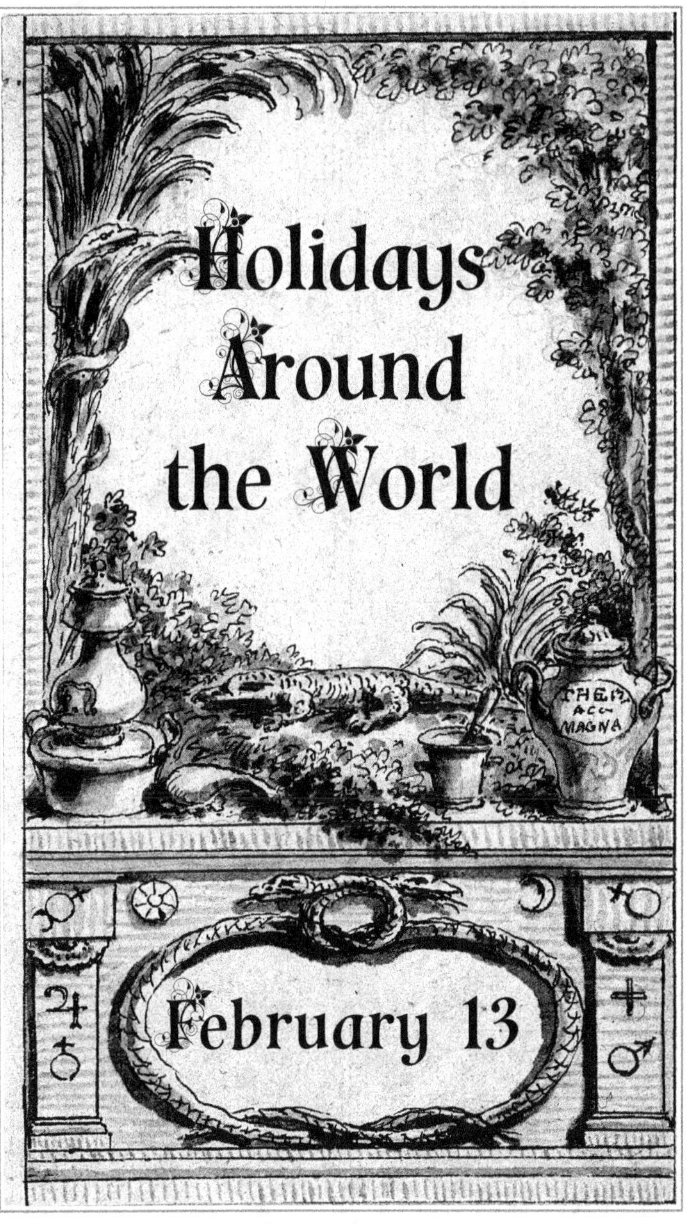

Holidays
Around
the World
February 13

Miss Rose Cade, "Queen of the Lemons," was nominated to be
southern California's "Swat the Jinx" girl in 1920

February 13 Holidays and Celebrations

If you're looking for a reason to take your special day off, you should know that every single day is a holiday somewhere in the world! Here's some of what you can celebrate on February 13!

Friday the Thirteenth

While February 13 doesn't come on Friday every year, sooner or later, every 13th day of the month eventually lands on the dreaded last day of the week.

Friday the 13th is considered an unlucky day in many (but not all) Western nations. Both the number 13 and Friday have a history of being thought unlucky, so when you put the two togethe.... The idea that Friday is unlucky seems to be a maritime superstition — sailors believed it was unlucky to start a voyage on a Friday.

As far as the number 13 goes, there are a number of theories.One theory is that it refers to the 13 people around the table at the Last Supper, one of whom (Judas) would shortly betray Jesus. Others point out that on Friday, October 13, 1307, the Knights Templar were arrested, and many of them were later tortured and killed. In Norse mythology, Loki becomes the 13th guest when he crashes a party in Valhalla; the fallout results in the death of Baldur.

Fear of the number thirteen is common enough that a psychological condition, *triskaidekaphobia,* is named for it! (Fear of Friday the 13th is *paraskevidekatriaphobia.*)

(Photo: W. J. Pilsak, CC BY-SA 3.0)

According to some researchers, between 17 and 21 million people in the US alone are bothered by Friday 13th. Fear of thirteen is so common that many tall buildings skip 13 when numbering floors — over 80 percent of high-rise buildings in the US alone! Many hotels, hospitals, and airports don't have rooms or gates numbered 13 either.

Perhaps some of the bad luck associated with Friday 13th is self-inflicted. Fewer people drive on Friday 13th, but there are more accidents.

In Spanish-speaking countries, as well as in Greece, they worry about Tuesday 13th (*martes trece*) instead —though either way, January 13 qualifies. In Italy, though, 13 is a lucky number — but watch out for Friday the 17th!

In most of Asia, the number four is considered unlucky — the Chinese words for "four" and "death" are similar. Buildings in Asia may have a 13th floor, but often don't have a 4th floor.

Black History Month

Important people and events in the African diaspora are commemorated during Black History Month (sometimes African-American History Month). In the US and Canada, Black History Month is observed in February; in the UK, it's October.

"The First Vote," by Alfred Waud (1867)

Mardi Gras

Mardi Gras, French for "Fat Tuesday," is also a religious celebration known as Shrove Tuesday.It celebration takes place the day before Ash Wednesday, the beginning of the Lenten season.

Mardi Gras can take place anywhere from February 3 to March 9 in regular years, and from February 4 to March 9 in leap years.

The New Orleans Mardi Gras celebration is perhaps the most famous, but Mardi Gras and the Carnival season (between Ephiphany and Ash Wednesday) are celebrated in many areas with large Catholic populations. It's known as *Karneval* or *Fasching* in Germany, *Martedi Grasso* in Italy, and *Fettisdagen* in Sweden.

Sheet music for the "Mardi Gras Rag," 1914

General Events

Children's Day (Myanmar)

Many nations set aside a day to celebrate children. The southeast Asian nation of Myanmar (formerly Burma) celebrates Children's Day on February 13.

World Radio Day (international)

The United Nations proclaimed World Radio Day to be held each February 13, to celebrate "the unique power of radio to touch lives and bring people together." The date was chosen to commemorate the anniversary of the 1946 establishment of United Nations Radio.

Food Holidays

In the United States, almost every day of the year is dedicated to a particular food — some days honor more than one!. (Other countries also have official food days, but not one for each day.) Sponsored by manufacturers, retailers, farmers, or simply fans, these days are often proclaimed by the President, Congress, state governors, or mayors.

In the US, February 13 is **National Italian Food Day.** There is a rich Italian heritage in the United States, and many traditionally Italian foods, ranging from spaghetti to pizza, are so common that they have become quintessential American foods as well.

In addition to celebrating Italian food overall, February 13 is also **National Tortellini Day**. Tortellini are ring-shaped pasta, typically stuffed with meat or cheese, originally from the Emilia region of Italy. Tortellini are also known as *ombelico* (belly button) because of their shape.

Tortellini (Photo: Cyclone Bill, CC BY-SA 2.0)

Honorary Food Months: In addition, the entire month of February is used to celebrate numerous foods. Here's a list of food-related observances in the month of February!

- Canned Food Month
- National Chocolate Lovers Month
- National Cherry Month
- National Grapefruit Month
- National Snack Food Month

- National Potato Lovers Month
- Return Shopping Carts to the Supermarket Month
- National Hot Breakfast Month

An abandoned shopping cart, by Michiel1972 (CC BY-SA 3.0) for RETURN SHOPPING CARTS TO THE SUPERMARKET MONTH

Religious Feast Days and Holidays

Ash Wednesday

Ash Wednesday, the day after Shrove Tuesday, begins the season of Lent, a period of prayer and self-denial commemorating the 40 days Jesus spent fasting in the desert, can begin any day between February 4 and March 10 in common years, and as late as March 11 in leap years. The exact beginning of Lent is calculated differently by different Christian denominations. *(Photo next page.)*

The Battle Between Carnival and Lent, by Jan Miense Molenaer

Saint Days

Each day in the year is considered a feast day for one or more saints. They are somewhat different in western Christianity (Catholicism and many forms of Protestantism) and in eastern (Orthodox) Christianity. There are many others; this is a selection.

In *Western Christianity*, February 13 is the feast day of Saints Absalom (Episcopal Church US), Beatrice of Ornacieux, Castor of Karden, Catherine of Ricci, Ermenilda of Ely, Fulcran, Jordan of Saxony, Polyeuctus (Roman Catholicism).

In *Eastern Orthodox Christianity*, it is also the commemoration of Saints Timothy of Alexandria, Julian of Lyons, Benignus of Todi, Stephen of Lyons, Modomnoc, Stephen of Rieti, Licinius of Angers, Huna of Thorney, Dyfnog, Aimo, Gosbert, Joseph of Volokolamsk, and Yurij Konissky. (These saints are honored on January 31 by "Old Calendrists.*")

Honorary Months

Presidents, Congresses, and nations around the world issue proclamations recognizing particular months to honor certain causes. These events generally fall in February, though honorary months do come and go.

Holidays established by states and nonprofit organizations are listed if verified. If not otherwise specified, all months are US. There is some variation from year to year; some celebratory months get added and others get dropped. Two places to get up to date information are the current edition of *Chase's Calendar of Events* or the website Brownielocks. Here are some honorary designations for February.

- American Heart Month
- International Month of Black Women in the Arts

---

* "Old Calendrists" use the older Julian calendar rather than the modern Gregorian calendar for liturgical purposes. February 13 on the Julian calendar is the same day as January 31 on the Gregorian calendar. For more about the different types of calendars, see "What Day of the Week is February 13?"

- International Prenatal Infection Prevention Month
- LGBT History Month (United Kingdom)
- Library Lovers Month
- Marijuana Awareness Month
- National Bird-Feeding Month
- National Condom Month
- National Children's Dental Health Month
- National Haiku Writing Month
- Pet Dental Health Month
- Season for Nonviolence (January 30-April 4, worldwide)
- Spunky Old Broads Month
- Youth Leadership Month

Moveable and Multi-Day Events

Some events take place over a specific week or time period. Start and finish dates may vary from year to year. Some events occur on different days each year (such as "fourth Saturday of a month"). These events sometimes take place on February 13.

Second Week in February

- National Marriage Week (US) — also Celebration of Love Week and Love Makes the World Go Round (but Laughter Keeps Us From Getting Dizzy) Week
- Children of Alcoholics Week
- International Friendship Week

- Random Acts of Kindness Week
- International Flirting Week (week including Valentine's Day)

Second Monday(February 8-14)

- Family Day (Canada)
- Meal Monday (Scotland)
- Clean Out Your Computer Week

Second Day of the Second Week (February 8-14)

- Safer Internet Day (international)

Second Tuesday (February 8-14)

- National Sports Day (Qatar)
- Extraterrestrial Culture Day

Second Saturday (February 8-14)

- International Purple Hijab Day

Second Sunday (February 8-14)

- Autism Sunday (United Kingdom)
- Children's Day (Cook Islands, Nauru, Niue, Tokelau, Cayman Islands)
- Mother's Day (Norway)
- World Marriage Day

Maagha (Hindu month, varies January/February)

- Ganesh Jayanti (Ganesha's Birthday)
- Ratha Saptami
- Vasant Panchami

Just for Fun

Anybody can make up a holiday, and many people do! While none of these are officially recognized and some may come and go, here are a few more holidays for February 13.

- Desperation Day
- Galentine's Day (day before Valentine's Day, created as part of the TV series *Parks and Recreation*)
- Get a Different Name Day
- International Condom Day
- National Wingman's Day

"February," by Eugène Grasset

Quote of the Day

"The most serious charge which can be brought against New England is not Puritanism but February."

Joseph Wood Krutch, critic, in *The Twelve Seasons* (1949)

About
the
Month
of
February
THER ACC MAGNA

 Michael Dobson

"February," from the *Brevarium Grimani* by Simon Bening (c.1510)

February: The Second Month

The February sunshine steeps your boughs
And tints the buds and swells the leaves within.
— *William Cullen Bryant, "Among the Trees"*

The month of February takes its name from the Latin word *februum*, meaning purification, because the traditional Roman festival Februa, involving ritual purification, took place in what we now know as mid-February each year.

Because the Romans considered winter to be a monthless period, neither January nor February existed in the Roman calendar until 713 BCE, and when February did become a month, it was the last month of the year!

The number of days in February also varied in ancient times because the calendar had to be periodically adjusted to stay in line with the seasons. In some years, it was only 23 days long. When the calendar and the seasons got too far out of alignment, the Romans added a bonus month, called Intercalaris, consisting of 27 days, to bring everything back on track.

Our modern month of February begins with the calendar reforms of Julius Caesar, known as the Julian[†] calendar. February became 28 days long, with an extra "leap day" added every four years.

[†] For an explanation of calendar types, see "What Day of the Week is February 13?"

Although the Julian calendar remained stable for a long time, it wasn't perfectly accurate, and the calendar gradually drifted away from the seasons again.

In 1582, under Pope Gregory XIII, the Julian calendar gave way to the Gregorian calendar, still in use today. One of the Gregorian reforms was to eliminate Leap Year when a new century was not divisible by four. As a result, 1800 and 1900 were leap years, but 2000 was not.

Although the pronunciation "feb-roo-err-ee" is preferred, the common pronunciation "feb-ew-err-ee" (as if the month was spelled "Feb-u-ary") is acceptable as well.

From the point of view of meteorologists, February is the third month of winter in the northern hemisphere and the third month of summer in the southern hemisphere.

February always starts on the same day of the week as March and November in common years, and on the same day as August in leap years. It ends on the same weekday as October in all years, and in common years also ends on the same weekday as January. In leap years, February is the only month that ends on the same day of the week as it began.

Because February is the only month with 28 days in common years, it is the only month that can pass without a single full moon. This happened in 1999 and will happen again in 2018. It is also the only month (in common years) that can have exactly four full 7-day weeks. This happens once every six years and twice every eleven years.

"February," by Joachim von Sandrart

February in Other Cultures

The month of February has different names in different languages. Some nations use calendars other than the Gregorian, and their months may overlap with February. In lunar-based calendars, such as the Islamic calendar, months move through the seasons. Still, many languages often have a word for February itself.

Albanian: Shkurt

Anglo-Saxon: Sol-monath (cake month)

Arabic (Egypt, Sudan, Yemen): يوناًغينافبراير (fibrāyir)

Arabic (Levant): حزيركانوشباط (shubāṭ)

Arabic (Libya): الصهناالنوار (an-nuwwār)

Arabic (Algeria and Tunisia): جأيفيفري (Fīfrī)

Arabic (Morocco): غينافبراير (fibrāyər)

Azerbaijani: Fevral

Basque: Otsail

Bulgarian: февруари (fevruari)

Chinese: 二月 (Cantonese: yihyuht; Mandarin: èryuè; Taiwanese: ji-goeh)

Corsican: Ferraghju

Croatian: Veljačaj

Czech: únor (month of submerging)

Finnish: Helmikuu (month of the pearl)

French: Février

German/Danish/Norwegian/Slovenian: Februar

Greek: Φεβρουάριος (Februoários)

Haitian Creole: Fevriye

Hebrew: ינפברואר (febru'ar)

Hindi: फ़रवरी (farvarī)

Hungarian: Február

Irish (Gaelic): Feabhra mí Feabhra

Italian: Febbraio

Japanese (traditional calendar): 二月 (nigatsu); 如月 (kisaragi)

Kazakh: Ақпан (Aḳpan)

Korean: 이월 (iweol)

Lithuanian: Vasaris

Maori: Hui tanguru

Old English: Solmōnaþ (mud month); Kale-monath (cabbage month)

Polish: Luty (month of ice)

Portuguese: Fevereiro

Russian: февраль (fevrali)

Scottish Gaelic: an Gearran

Sesotho: Hlakola

Spanish: Febrero

Swahili/Dutch/Swedish: Februari

Swazi: iNdlovana

Thai: Kumphaphan

Turkish: şubat

Ukrainian: лютий (ljutyj) (month of hard frost)

Vietnamese: 腈台 (tháng ha)

Walloon: Fevrî

Welsh: Chwefror

Yiddish: פעברואַר (februar)

Zulu: uFebruwari

February Sayings and Superstitions

Here are some sayings and superstitions associated with the month of February.

February Weather Superstitions

February 12 to 14 were said to be "borrowed" from January. If those days were stormy, the year would have good weather, but if they were clear, the rest of the year would be foul.

When the cat lies in the sun in February/She will creep behind the stove in March.

Of all the months of the year/Curse a fair February.

If it thunders in February, it will frost in April.

If February give much snow/A fine summer it doth foreshow

February Wedding Superstitions

A February bride will be an affectionate wife/ And a tender mother.

Married in February's sleepy weather/Life you'll tread in time together.

When February birds do mate/You wed nor dread your fate.

In Morocco, there is a ban on marriage during the seven days of *hesoum* (February 24 to March 4)

Valentine's Day Superstitions

The first man an unmarried woman sees on February 14 will be her future husband.

On Valentine's Day, if a girl writes all the names of her suitors on paper, wraps them in clay, and puts them in water, the piece that rises to the top first is the name of her husband to be.

If a woman sees a robin flying overhead on Valentine's Day, she will marry a sailor. If she sees a sparrow, she will marry a poor man but be very happy. If she sees a goldfinch, she will marry a rich person (happiness not guaranteed).

Leap Year Superstitions

Traditionally, women can propose to men on leap days, because the day had no legal status and therefor traditions did not apply. At one time, there was a Scottish law forbidding a man to refuse such a proposal. To ensure success, women should wear a red petticoat under their dress—and make sure it's partially visible to the man when they propose.

In some European countries, if a man refuses a woman's proposal on February 29, he must buy her 12 pairs of gloves.

In Scotland, it's considered unlucky to be born on a Leap Year's Day. Greeks consider it unlucky to be married during a leap year, and especially on a leap day. If you divorce during a leap year, you will never find happiness again.

February Symbols

Birthstone: Amethyst, representing piety, humility, spiritual wisdom, and sincerity

Birth Flowers: Violet and Primrose

Soviet postage stamp of an amethyst from the 1963 "Precious Stone of the Urals" series

Violet (Photo: Andrew Bossi CC BY-SA 2.5)

Still life (primroses, pears, and pomegranates),
by Henri Fantin-Latour

"February," by Hans Thoma

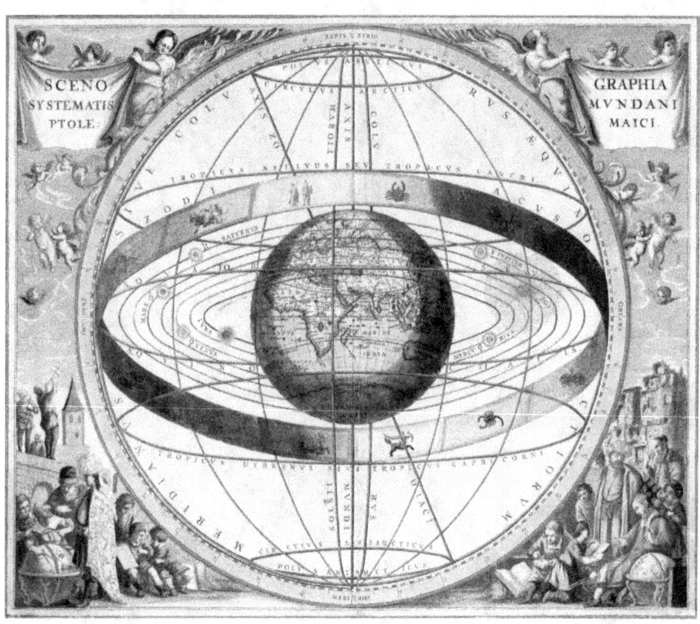

Scenography of the Ptolemaic Cosmography, by Johannes van Loon, based on Andreas Cellarius's *Harmonia Macrocosmica,* 1660

February 13 Zodiac Signs

From the perspective of someone on Earth, the Sun appears to move through the sky throughout the year, along a path astronomers call the *ecliptic plane*. The ecliptic plane is divided into twelve constellations, known as the zodiac, based on traditionally observed patterns of stars. On your birthday, you can't see your constellation, because it's in the daytime sky.

The zodiac was first developed by Babylonian astronomers about 2,500 years ago. Because they were unaware that the Earth wobbles like a spinning top (known as *precession*), they didn't make allowance for the fact that the Sun's path through the zodiac changes over time.

That means there are now two sets of dates for your birth sign. The *tropical dates* are the original Babylonian dates; the *sidereal dates* tell you where the Sun actually appears as it moves along its annual path.

For February 13, the tropical sign is **Aquarius** and the sidereal sign is **Capricorn.**

Aquarius

Tropical January 20 to February 19
Sidereal February 12 to March 8 (March 9 in leap years)

Aquarius is one of the oldest recognized constellations, originally representing the Babylonian god Ea. In Latin, Aquarius means "water-carrier," represented in its symbol. In Greek mythology, Aquarius is sometimes associated with Deucalion, who survived a world-cleansing flood. In Chinese astronomy, it is known as the Black Tortoise of the North (北方玄武, Běi Fāng Xuán Wǔ).

In astrology, Aquarius is considered to be masculine and extroverted, and despite the name is an air sign. Aquarians are supposed to be philanthropical, inventive, and individualistic.

Capricorn

Tropical December 22 to January 20
Sidereal January 15 to February 14

The origins of the constellation Capricorn date back to Sumeria and Babylonia. Based on Enki, the Sumerian god of wisdom and waters, Capricorn has the head and upper body of a mountain goat and the lower body and tail of a fish. The mountain goat represents ambition and intelligence, the fish represents passion and spirituality.

An earth sign, Capricorn is ruled by the planet Saturn. They are often thought to be responsible, patient, ambitious and loyal, but can sometimes be seen as conceited, distrusting, and unimaginative. Capricornians are supposed to be compatible with Taurus, Pisces, and Virgo, but not with Aries, Sagittarius, or Leo.

Illustration by Edward Penfield

What Day of the Week is February 13?

On what day of the week does February 13 fall?

Surprisingly, this isn't an easy question. Because the calendar year is 365 days long (366 in leap years), it doesn't divide evenly by the seven days of the week.

Also, the Earth goes around the Sun in about 365-1/4 days, so a calendar tends to drift over time. That's why the same date falls on different weekdays in different years.

This is made even more complicated by a change in calendars that took place in 1582. Our modern calendar has its roots in ancient Rome, in a calendar reform conducted by Julius Caesar. Caesar commissioned mathematicians to attack the problem, and they came up with the idea of leap years, and thus standardized the calendar for centuries to come. This was called the Julian calendar.

Over time, however, the small errors in Caesar's calculation compounded. That's why Pope Gregory XIII commissioned the Gregorian calendar, used in most of the world today. Some countries converted in 1582, when the calendar was first developed; some converted later; other still haven't changed.

Gregorian and Julian aren't the only types of calendars. The Hebrew year, the Islamic year, and many other calendars are used in different parts of the world and among different people.

You can convert Gregorian dates to other calendars, including the Hebrew calendar, the Islamic calendar, and even the Mayan calendar by visiting the Fourmilab Calendar Converter at http://www.fourmilab.ch/documents/calendar/.

Chinese calendar systems are quite complex and have changed several times; a full discussion is far beyond the scope of this book. If you're interested, you can find information here: http://www.hermetic.ch/cal_stud/chinese_cal.htm.

On Names and Dates

Historians use "CE" (Common Era) and "BCE" (Before the Common Era) instead of the more common "AD" (Anno Domini, or Year of Our Lord) and "BC" (Before Christ), reflecting the fact that the year-numbering system established by the Gregorian calendar is used throughout the world in many countries not culturally Christian.

The CE/BCE designation dates back to at least 1708, and has been adopted as a standard by the United Nations and the Universal Postal Union. Because this series of books covers events and people of all nations and cultures, we use the CE/BCE terms.

The abbreviation "O.S." ("Old Style") and "N.S." ("New Style") on some dates refers to the fact that the Russian Empire (in particular) did not switch from the Julian to the Gregorian calendar at the same time as the rest of Europe, and therefore some figures and events have two dates.

Also, in the Julian calendar in England in the 16th century, the year began on March 25 rather than January 1. To avoid confusion with Gregorian dates, dates between January and March were often written using both years.

People and events whose original names are not in the Western alphabet have their native names (where possible) in the appropriate script shown in parenthesis. If you are using an e-reader to access an electronic version of this book, all characters don't always display on all devices.

A 50-year brass perpetual calendar.

Quote of the Day

"Time is an illusion, lunchtime doubly so."

Douglas Adams,
from *The Hitchhiker's Guide to the Galaxy*

Notes
and
Credits
THE.M
ACC·
MAGNA
Timespinner
Press

Cartoon by John T. McCutcheon

Copyright, Credit, and Contact

Follow Us

Our blog "This Day in History" (http:// timespinnerpress.com/this-day-in-history/) features short articles on events and people associated with each day, and updates several times each week. Also subscribe to the "Quote of the Day" at http://timespinnerpress.com/quote-of-the-day/. You can get daily links by following us on Facebook at TimespinnerPress, or on Twitter as @sidewisethinker.

Contact Us

Find an error or a format problem? Want information about the series, about us, or about when the volume for your special day might be available? Please email us at editor@timespinnerpress.com. (We also take requests if your special day isn't yet complete. Please give us at least six weeks' notice if possible.)

Sources

We owe a great debt to Wikipedia, which is our first stop for research. We attempt to make independent confirmation of all important dates and facts through a variety of other sources.

Other sources we frequently use include the Library of Congress; "on this day" listings from *Encyclopedia Britannica,* the *New York Times,* and the BBC; Omniglot for the names of months in other languages; *Chase's Calendar of Events;* and, of course, the always essential Google.

All art and photographs are either in the public domain, used under a Creative Commons license, or with a "fair use" justification, and most frequently come from Wikimedia Commons and the Library of Congress Prints and Photographs Division.

Attribution is provided where possible, or as requested by the copyright owner, or when there is particular historical significance, listed below. For information about any particular illustration or photograph, please contact us.

Credits

1. The cover photograph of the St. Louis Giants National Negro League team was taken in 1916 by the Star Photo Company, and is in the public domain because its copyright has expired. It is from the collection of the Missouri History Museum, GUID 68470924-1FCA-9538-A4FD-D65805F5424F.

2. The illustration of the month of February used on the back cover is from the French Gothic illuminated manuscript *Les Très Riches Heures du duc de Berry* by the Limbourg Brothers, Jean Colombe, and an intermediate painter whose name is lost to history. It is in the public domain because its copyright has expired.

3. The box graphic used on the first page is from a 1916 pamphlet entitled "Divorce versus Democracy" authored by G. K. Chesterton, originally published in London by the Society of St. Peter and St. Paul. It is in the public domain in the US because it was published prior to 1923, and is in the public domain in all countries (including the country of origin) in which the copyright time is the author's life plus 70 years or less.

4. The graphic design for the section pages in this book is from a design originally created for a pharmacy label. It is courtesy of Wellcome Images (ICV No 11073, photo V0010813), and is used here under CC BY-SA 4.0.

5. The 1646 portrait of Catherine Howard by Wenceslas Hollar is from the Thomas Fisher Rare Book Library. It is in the public domain because its copyright has expired.

6. The 1890 drawing of the Cuban Giants was originally published in the Cleveland *Gazette*. It is in the public domain because its copyright has expired.

7. The photograph of the 1922 Dixie World Series is by David Sedman and originally appeared in the Dallas *Express*. It is in the public domain because its copyright has expired.

8. The pages from Leonardo da Vinci's *Madrid Codices* were created circa 1493, and are in the public domain because their copyright has expired. The originals are from the collection of the Biblioteca Nacional de España.

9. The 1938 photograph of Robert H. Jackson is by Harris & Ewing, courtesy Library of Congress digital ID cph.3b04770. According to the Library, there are no known copyright restrictions on the use of this work.

10. The 1930 painting *American Gothic* by Grant Wood is in the public domain because it was published in the United States between 1923 and 1963, and although there may or may not have been a copyright notice, the copyright was not renewed. The original is in the collection of the Art Institute of Chicago. It is used here courtesy Google Art Project.

11. The 2008 photograph of a motorcycle built from Erector Set/ Mecchano parts was created by Essig, who released the work into the public domain.

12. The 1952 photograph of the Trumans by Abbie Rowe is courtesy of the Harry S. Truman Library, NARA record 8451352. It is in the public domain as a work created by an employee of the US government as part of that person's official duties.

13. The 1833 portrait of Robert Malthus by John Linnell is in the public domain because its copyright has expired.

14. The photograph of Chuck Yeager and the Bell X-1 is in the public domain as a work created by an employee of the US government as part of that person's official duties. The photograph has been cropped.

15. The 1966 publicity photograph of the Monkees is in the public domain because it was first published in the United States between 1923 and 1977 without a copyright notice. Traditionally, publicity photographs are not copyrighted because of the way in which they are intended to be used.

16. The 1957 publicity photograph of Tennessee Ernie Ford is in the public domain because it was first published in the United States between 1923 and 1977 without a copyright notice. Traditionally, publicity photographs are not copyrighted because of the way in which they are intended to be used.

17. The 1965 publicity photograph of Carol Lynley is in the public domain because it was first published in the United States between 1923 and 1977 without a copyright notice. Traditionally, publicity photographs are not copyrighted because of the way in which they are intended to be used.

18. The 1962 publicity photograph of Kim Novak by Frank Bez is from the private collection of Kim Novak, and released by them for public use. It is in the public domain because it was first published in the United States between 1923 and 1977 without a copyright notice.

19. The 1915 publicity photograph from *A Midsummer Night's Dream* is is in the public domain because it was first published in the United States between 1923 and 1977 without a copyright notice. Traditionally, publicity photographs are not copyrighted because of the way in which they are intended to be used.

20. The 2009 photograph of Randy Moss is used under CC BY-SA 2.0.

21. The 1963 publicity photograph of David Janssen in *The Fugitive* is in the public domain because it was first published in the United States between 1923 and 1977 without a copyright notice. Traditionally, publicity photographs are not copyrighted because of the way in which they are intended to be used.

22. The 1887 painting "Early Spring in Glostrup" by Albert Gottschalk is in the collection of the National Gallery of Denmark. It is in the public domain because its copyright has expired.

23. The 1550 drawing of Benvenuto Cellini is in the public domain because its copyright has expired.

24. The 1935 publicity photograph of Lily Pons by Ernest Bacharach is in the public domain because it was first published in the United States between 1923 and 1977

without a copyright notice. Traditionally, publicity photographs are not copyrighted because of the way in which they are intended to be used.

25. The 1915 publicity photograph of Mae Marsh in *The Birth of a Nation* is in the public domain because its copyright has expired.

26. The portrait of Cotton Mather by Peter Pelham was created circa 1700, and is in the public domain because its copyright has expired.

27. The 1866 painting "February in the Isle of Wight" by John Brett is in the public domain because its copyright has expired. The image is courtesy Google Art Project; the original can be found in the Birmingham Museum and Art Gallery.

28. The 1920 photograph of Miss Rose Cade is from the Keystone View Company. It is in the public domain because its copyright has expired.

29. The photograph of a calendar showing Friday the 13th was taken by W. J. Pilsak, and is used here under CC BY-SA 3.0)

30. The illustration "The First Vote" by Alfred R. Waud originally appeared on the cover of *Harper's* magazine in 1867. It is in the public domain because its copyright has expired.

31. The sheet music cover for the 1914 song "Mardi Gras Rag", by Lyons and Yosco, was published by Geo. W. Meyer Music Co., New York. It is in the public domain because it was first published prior to January 1, 1923.

32. The 2013 photograph of tortellini is by Cyclone Bill, and is used here under CC BY-SA 2.0.

33. The photograph of an abandoned shopping cart is by Michiel1972, and is used here under CC BY-SA 3.0.

34. The painting The Battle Between Carnival and Lent by Jan Miense Molenaer was painted between 1633 and 1634, and is in the public domain because its copyright has expired. It is in the collection of the Indianapolis Museum of Art.

35. The 1896 drawing "February" by Eugène Grasset is in the public domain because its copyright has expired.

36. The painting "February" is from the *Brevarium Grimani*, circa 1510, and is in the public domain because its copyright has expired.

37. The painting "February" by Joachim von Sandrart is in the public domain because its copyright has expired. The original can be found in the Staatsgalerie im Neuen Schloss, Schleißheim, Germany.

38. The 1815 woodcut of a proposal is in the public domain because its copyright has expired.

39. The 1963 Soviet postage stamp of an amethyst from the "Precious Stones of the Urals" series is not an object of copyright according to article 1259 of Book IV of the Civil Code of the Russian Federation No. 230-FZ, 12/18/2006.

40. The photograph of violets at the Abbey Church of Saint Peter, Salzburg, Austria, was taken by Andrew Bossi and used here under CC BY-SA 2.5.

41. The painting *"Nature morte (primevères, poires et grenades)"* by Henri Fantin-Latour is in the public domain because its copyright has expired. The original can be found at the Kröller-Müller Museum, Otterlo, Netherlands. Image courtesy Google Art Project by way of Wikimedia Commons.

42. The illustration "February" by Hans Thoma is from his book *Festkalendar*, and is in the public domain because it was first published prior to January 1, 1923.

43. The celestial sphere is from *Scenography of the Ptolemaic Cosmography*, by Johannes van Loon, based on Andreas Cellarius's *Harmonia Macrocosmica*, 1660. It is in the public domain because its copyright has expired.

44. The 1906 automobile calendar is by Edward Penfield, and is in the collection of the Library of Congress Prints and Photographs Division. It is in the public domain because its copyright has expired.

45. The 50-year perpetual calendar photograph is in the public domain.

46. The cartoon by John T. McCutcheon is from his 1905 collection *The Mysterious Stranger and Other Cartoons by John T. McCutcheon*. It is in the public domain because its copyright has expired.

License Description and Terms

Aside from material purely in the public domain, photographs and other material in this book are used under specific licenses permitting free use, usually with an attribution requirement. For full text and terms of these licenses, click or enter the appropriate links below. If you believe there is an error in the copyright status or attribution of any of these images, please email us.

- Creative Commons Attribution 2.0 Generic (CC-BY 2.0): http://creativecommons.org/licenses/by/2.0/deed.en
- Creative Commons Attribution-Share Alike 3.0 Generic (CC-BY-SA 3.0): http://creativecommons.org/licenses/by-sa/3.0/
- Creative Commons Attribution-Share Alike 2.5 Generic (CC-BY-SA 2.5): http://creativecommons.org/licenses/by-sa/2.5/deed.en
- Creative Commons Attribution-Share Alike 2.0 Generic (CC-BY-SA 2.0): http://creativecommons.org/licenses/by/2.0/deed.en
- Creative Commons Attribution-Share Alike 1.0 Generic (CC-BY-SA 1.0): http://creativecommons.org/licenses/by-sa/1.0/deed.en
- CC0 1.0 Universal (CC0 1.0) Public Domain Dedication (CC0 1.0) http://creativecommons.org/publicdomain/zero/1.0/deed.en
- GNU Free Documentation License (GFDL): http://en.wikipedia.org/wiki/Wikipedia:Text_of_the_GNU_Free_Documentation_License
- License Art Libre (Free Art License): http://artlibre.org

Other Books from Timespinner Press

The Story of a Special Day
Michael Dobson

A series of (eventually) 366 volumes covering everything that happened on your special day! Events, births, deaths, quotes, holidays, and much more. It's like a birthday card they'll never throw away!

US$7.95 print/US$2.99 ebook.

From Plassey to Pakistan
Humayun Mirza

The history of British Colonial India and the formation of Pakistan from the unique perspective of the son of Pakistan's first president and last of the royal line of Bengal, Bihar, and Orissa! This unique historical document tells the inside story of this distinguished family, including the detailed story of the coup that toppled his father from power!

US$27.95 print

A Whole New Navy: America's War in the Pacific

Miles Durr

The most comprehensive and detailed description of America's naval war in the Pacific ever—every battle, every ship, every task force and every task group from Pearl Harbor through the Japanese surrender! A must-have for the collection of every World War II buff!

US$29.95 print

Improbable History: The Weird, the Obscure, and the Strangely Important

edited by Michael Dobson

From the birth of Western civilization to the rescue of Apollo 13, from the Leaning Tower of Pisa to Florence's Duomo, history has often turned on small, improbable details. Whatever happened to the ancient Samaritan people? Why did a fortuitous rainstorm allow the British to conquer India? How did an air raid in Italy lead to the development of chemotherapy? What happened when Albert Einstein met Adolf Hitler on the streets of Berlin? How did the Japanese manage to attack the US mainland using balloons? A cast of award-winning writers tackle some of the strangest tales in history!

US$19.95 print

The Letters of William Philip Schwartz 1842-1855

edited by John F. Schwartz

The 19th century soldier and adventurer William Philip Schwartz wrote a series of vivid and detailed letters chronicling his adventures in the Indian Wars, the Mexican-American War, the Gold Rush, and his term as Marine sergeant aboard the USS Constellation. A pioneer in photography, he took *the first known war photographs*. An unforgettable first-hand look into life in the 19th century!

US$17.95 print

Timespinner
Press

www.timespinnerpress.com

www.ingramcontent.com/pod-product-compliance
Lightning Source LLC
Chambersburg PA
CBHW070818240726
48654CB00007B/399